AF333612

milk tooth bane bone

milk

tooth

bane

bone

daniela elza

leaf press

Library and Archives Canada Cataloguing in Publication

Elza, Daniela, 1967-

   Milk tooth bane bone / Daniela Elza.

Poems.

ISBN 978-1-926655-60-4

   I. Title.

PS8609.L93M55 2013   C811'.6   C2013-901350-4

Editor for the title: Aislinn Hunter
Introduction copyright © 2013 by Aislinn Hunter

We gratefully acknowledge the support of the Canada Council for the Arts
and the British Columbia Arts Council.

Grateful as well for permissions to use the following:

Cover painting by Seth Elza.
Crow photograph used as an ornament by Greg Pond.
Crow photographs on the section pages by Daniela Elza.
Author photo by Frank Lee.

Printed in Canada on FSC certified papers.
Set in Minion Pro.

Leaf Press
Box 416
Lantzville, BC, Canada
V0R 2H0

for what fuels the imagination

for the child we only half see
for you, and always
for suddenly, and all at once

:contents:

In *A Short History of Myth* Karen Armstrong notes that one of the qualities of a myth is that it looks into the heart of a great silence. Daniela Elza's book of poetry, with its silences and fissures and gaps, its trickster crow, its broken/open semiotics and its hauntings reminds me of a myth, of that attempt to construct the self through utterances and story. That said, the wonder of these poems is the celebratory feel of them, the poet's willingness to throw herself into the search, as if there might be a magic word out there that will call all the properties of the self into cohesion. Myths, of course, are also attached to place, are formed, in many ways, out of the landscape and resources and metaphysics of a particular location. In *milk tooth bane bone* "place" is as unseated as the crows that swoop through many of these poems and flit in and out of the poet's consciousness. When you have lived on three continents, when you speak more than one language, when places as diverse as Bulgaria, Nigeria, England, the United States and Canada have been called, however briefly, *home*, how is one to tell the myth of one's place in the world? Through the fragment perhaps, through the constancy of a bird, through whatever coattails of story your family has bequeathed you. This is not to tie the poems in this collection too tightly to the biography of the poet, only to suggest that what is at work here, in these wonderful poems, seems to me to come from a very deep place, but also from a sense of no place or displacement—a rich interstice that is perhaps more strongly represented in the poetic tradition of other nations, although the lyric philosophy of some of our finest Canadian poets is changing that.

The construction and deconstruction of a personal mythology is a powerful theme, but what I admire about this book is that as it works through "the rattle of logic" and "the edge   between   substance / and / nothingness" it also grapples with language itself—the very tool of meaning-making employed here. In this way words themselves are queried, broken open or exposed in the same way our crows break open mussels with their beaks. In a similar

vein the crows themselves shape-shift. Yes, they are crows
but sometimes they are other things: a crowsmos, a story,
language itself, the in*substantial*, the paradoxical. What Elza
creates in much of this work is a purposeful slippage — of
language, of things, of history, of self. Jane Hirshfield once
suggested that "[p]oetry's work is the clarification and
magnification of being." Elza's work seems to support this
principle, but at no point in this book does she pretend that
such a task can ever be straight-ahead or simple.

What struck me on rereading this collection was how wholly
it is also about community. In a book of poetry that so openly
engages with semiotics and language (Elza has a degree in
philology), this might be easy to miss. First there are the host
of writers, philosophers and poets whose ideas Elza cites,
or whose words Elza folds into her own thinking, but there
is also a "we" here — familial, generational, but also, more
expansively, human, and sometimes, pan-ecological — a we
that includes crow and land. It's been said that in a post-
modern world one ought not to use "we" because subjectivity
and difference make "we" impossible. This may be one of the
reasons I have been such a fan of Daniela's work from the
beginning, because I think this idea is wrong, that sometimes
"we" is a good place to start, because it conveys a kind of
optimism, because in tandem with the "I it can function as
a kind of call, as the extension of a hand. This is what I love
about this book: that the work takes me somewhere, that it
asks me questions, and offers me ideas.

In "the crow hour" Elza puts it this way:

this   :all of a sudden: I know.
this   :I am not alone: here.

and poetry?   what can it do
before we awake?   but take us   part way

Aislinn Hunter
Vancouver, 2013

"Ah, whom can we ever turn to
in our need? Not angels, not humans,
and already the knowing animals are aware
that we are not really at home in
our interpreted world."

–Rainer Maria Rilke

:pre*face*:

"The World is a semantic sign
that cannot be pronounced."
–Lyubomir Levchev

today   a crow   flies up.
a mussel in its beak.

        drops it.
        repeats.

        I pick up a word.

        drop it.

      and again

    to see it

crack.

      we look   at each other
sideways   crow & I

for an instant   agree—   this kind of
        sustenance *is*   miserable.

    yet   with unexpected
      concentration

we resume   our e*fforts*.

:dia*gnosis*:

"Language is what something becomes
when you think in it."
–Robert Bringhurst

the snow   settled thick   on the branches.

so quiet

          (it could have been   )

the pin-   point   of light

                              in the eye

          watching

without a trace   a crow

                flies away.

                  another

takes its place.   on the gallows

                the noose is not

                        empty.

winter footsteps

          filled with

                the need for light.

the crows   could be

             the bitter fruit of trees

lining this field of   stark

                contrasts.

                  so still

(as if

      what has fallen   is not

                      :snow:

from this far
            from this end of the field
                                    pages flutter
  into   *memory*   )
)
)
  with   my eyes   half closed
                            even the gallows appear

        to have always been   there.

                                    crows

take turns   passing on   sharp-
                                    eyed   secrets.

the letters—   faceless.
                            ink
                            caught heavy

                        in the mind's gravity.

                named   crows   turning

        white.   as black   snow

falls   on   deaf ears.

a field of snow. a picture   of a tree.
the body hangs.   a eulogy.

suspended   groundless   words fall
around   a simple question

                              (at first sight

black   on white)   so clearly
outlined—   a tree   a body

and a breath   between them.

                    *

and the crows   they utter   their deadly caws
all at once   (as if   trying

to explain.

                              they saw it all

with their sharp little eyes   but none
swooped down   to blind   the executioner.

*

their cawing   grows
                    especially loud

at dusk   when I hang   by that thin

noose
        of dying

        light.

                        alone.

:axiom:
the *call*ing

"As the eye cannot see itself directly
But only in reflection
So also does consciousness appear
Mirrored in the ten thousand things."

in ot*her* wor[1]ds   icicles me[1]t

                reflecting

their past   snowf[1]ake-   selves.

a crow   cuts through
a fan of sudden light.   [1]ands

on a laden branch.   does not see   itself

fal[1]ing upside down.
                                        d
                                        r
                                        o
                                        p

                                        by
                                        drop.

after the demolition   and the fear

        there was   a faërie-ness
              about the ruins.

> "It happened in the theatre of the trees,
> the hovering of shadow, the telos of snow."
> –Ross Leckie

the snowflake: a case study

you tell me of   the beginning—

in the heat of the kitchen

                                        we scoop
two tablespoons of
                    wood ash.
                                        whisk them
in water   to make sweets.

not a bit nervous

                    under my child gaze

                                        you tell me   how

I arrived

how I lifted
            from forests
                        from lakes

                        (stirred by
                        dendrite reflections of trees)

how I
            crystallized
                        around
                                    ancestral dust—

a fractal—

how I landed   on your September windowsill

and how   you
                 brought me

in.

                         *
                             *

I watched   outside
                         the thick snow flitting on

my thoughts.
                 imagined   what it took

                                        to wrench myself
                             out of
                     a carapace
             of ice—

the coat of arms

                 that gripped   the thorax.

did not buckle at
                     the inconsistencies.

your voice
                 carried   its own

proof.

* *
 *

in time
                    the rattle of logic   cracked

my fr*agile* story—

              its vessel fis*sure*d
                                    with doubt:

          why *snowflake*?
                              why not *seashell*?

or   a *blade of grass*?

I watched the lattice of my tale

          coll*apse*—

                                              a coat

                    I slowly shed

          as I picked apart

          its woven strands.

(*wait a minute:*   *snow?*   *in September?*

among its shades of raw
                              to burnt sienna
there is no such white
                    no place for it to land.)

                                        *

                          *   *

                            *

                                          one day I follow
                      the fi*lament* of time
            stretching   back
nine months
before.

          falling
                    in the month of January.
                                (which makes more
                                        sense

but never settles

              my c o n c e p t i o n:

this crystal
                          *me*mory of   (being

                                            caught
                                            wondering

what it felt like   to be   air born.

such knowing is
                              a loss   I have
              to mourn—

the way a snowflake lands
and only once
                              among the ashes
                                on our tongues.

today   a dot of

                                .

                                                    ink

                    becomes   the particle
around which thought begins

  to form
                    *

f i l a g r e e   lattices
        * .   * .
    *   * .   *
  * .   * .   *   * .   *
                    they tumble out of
                                    air's symmetry
                *

                                out of nothing
            out of chaos

out of order

as if).   (locked in reason-
                                    able
            geometries

        they   create
                  delineate
                  ignite

a wor(l)d.

spring.
                words

                                    everywhere—
in the pines
            on lampposts

                                            strung

on wires.
            cawing me

                                out of my *skin*.

so close
            I look them

                                        in the eye

down by   the g*rates*   the gar*bage*.

on the edge of the water
                            they shine
(mussels)—
                        a w*hole* murder of them.

so blue-black   you would   think

                    they are standing   in rain.

picking th*oughts*   *clean*.

winter leaves
                   still

                                      fly around—

their skeletons

                   float   on water   (as if
ghost hands   reaching

some   rest on the backs of   barnacles
searching.   bleached.

some   you could swear
                                     look

like the beginnings of

                        crows' feet.

at.tension

I cannot draw   these crows.
they speak: crow   on snow.

peck their way   in and out   of p*lots*
I cannot

                follow.

up there
          on the lamppost   a word
sepa*rates* us.   falls.   empty.

opaque. dissolves   on a sunlit wing.

                *

in the lymph light   they ripple
in the *frantic* search   for a morsel.

as the tide goes out
                we follow
                        its footprints—
the raw flesh

          it leaves

behind.

why crows
                you ask?

here   there are other birds too—

seagulls   cormorants   herons.

                it doesn't always have to be

a crow.

                but
                I notice   crows—

the pin-point   of light

                in the eye

that watches
                me

                        watching.

as a child I would hear them   at dawn
in my bed   on the eighth floor

(imagine them   all huddled around
chimneys   and   TV antennas

          (a chorus

high above   the winter city.
at such a tender time

          I could even   hear them
through the thinning walls of   dreams

just before   the first high heels

          clatter

     onto the morning pavement.

today the crow in the pine is   a story—
its harsh   charred voice   pulls the morning

out of the water.   *ripples*
the city's dissolving   *dreams.*

they walk in broad daylight th*rough* memory
lanes   lined   with walls so thin

you can see   where the dumpsters used to be

benches
                where we sat and held hands.

under the water   a book   turning pages.
slow   words   come undone

float to the surface black   oily   and slick.
flow under bridges   arches   aches

the m*arrow* of the quiet   the writing down
and what a crow tears   out of

                        such silence.

I write between drops.   eaves dripping.
two crows in a tree   like ears   listen.

again   I fool myself
                    that I can even get close
                              to writing   :rain:

these   *ghosts* on the page that pull at me
drag me out of my *skin*   into certainties.

if we have to be   truly philosophical
                                        we will not say

a word.

          in the linden tree   below the balcony—

the breaking of twigs   the weaving of a nest.

crows here   speak so effortlessly   of rain
tap   tapping   on leaves

and the *strip* of light   above the horizon
a*gain*
          delivers us
                    to the eye of the moon
                                        to the night

where we are   dark thought   perched
in the trees of dreams.

with first light
        you notice
                speckled turquoise eggs.

     rain   isn't
                divisible   from this.

my father tells me: as a child
he pulled his sled   along the train tracks.
he and his friends. looked for   (black)

coal nesting in the snow.   they gather
every speck they find.   pile it
on their sleds   carefully   lined with

newspaper   so nothing would fall out
between   small footprints   between
narrow sled rails. they would even scoop up

the dust   that fell   when the coal-
trains   rattled   through   their town.

only when he   brought coal   home
was there   a fire   to sit around.

what he held   was not   coal.

he held   the tongues   of flames
burning stories   through
his thick   woollen   mittens.

grandmother

you picked nettles.		the tender ones
grew in the shade of trees.			without a doubt

picked them	with your bare hands.	cooked them
with rice			and white cheese.

your hands	(the smell of them)
held seamless		the sirens		the shelters
				the shrapnel	the lack.

deep shadows—		the shape of crows' feet—
		cool with		splintered
conversations.		questions			broken

before I could ask.		snapped		their tender tips
with your:		*don't look back*

how I loved a bird   once   with a hug
sotightitstoppedbreathing.

held it   in my toddler hands
set it down on the lid of a barrel in the backyard.

poked it   (hoping)
                  to spur it   back
into life.

it lay there   thinner
                   (all the while)
                             its eye fixed on me.

that afternoon at three
my grandmother's neighbour made me   (feel)

a murderer   as she leaned over the garden sink
plucked that chicken   for dinner.

at feeding time   they gather
            in the birches.   circle.
                        mussels in their beaks.

        my path littered with
                broken shells.

the splash of   sea water
            on   winter   pavement.

an instant's sleek shadow
            across   my face

                pecks a memory
                            out of my eye.

two ravens raise a raucous in a nearby tree
above the construction site   outside the city.

I have never heard   ravens say   so much.

in the morning he insists   by the motel window
an argument   made over   and over.

Being   is no amount   of narration.

the words with their hems undone   (as if
each one   a poem

                    the poem

always
                    an approximation.

walls pressed   between us
thinning   with memory   you can almost

            see through: navigate time as

(we become
irrelevant.   so   what   if

a crow flies   into my mind?
I can try   and ignore it.   focus   on some

mundane task—   dusting   chopping

washing.   pretend
the bird is   not there.

then turn the corner   go through
another wall.

            black wings   nailed
above the place   that marks   (the en*trance*.

some days I am too empty   for de*scriptions*.
myths span our   damp sky   with doubt.

                                        we look at

each other—   negatives of   ourselves.
crumbs tossed in   axioms of sorrow

and so
          I watch your mouth   become

               a crow-shaped
               black hole.

my gaze   pulled tight   around
the edge   between   substance

                              and

                              nothingness.

between what stutters   into night
                    what splinters into   morning.

they   perch behind   my ear.
nest there   in my hair.

their carrion breath   permeates
the spaces   between.   temples

full   of restless

     wings.

a place turned so black
I could   mistake it for

          grief

and my child

      sits poised with   the brush
ready   for the first   stroke.   up.

down.   a crow flaps   closer.
watching.   sideways

stroke
and the character   is taking shape.

my son

he sees the crow.   begins   to move
a brush   with some other

consciousness   at work.

the crow   and the boy   caught

in   the song   of being

                between them

on other days   they settle with such ease—
ink   in white   birches.

among first cherry blossoms
they exchange places.   swaying

in the paper-   thin wind   (as if
unaware   of the contrasts

                          they create.

I may not even be   an impulse
in their shiny   mussel eye

as they lift up   the crowns   of trees.
in each claw—   a piece of sky.

:method:
*quest*ioning

"The half seen thing
   a snare that baits us with desire."
                              –Aislinn Hunter

"the memory dreams, and reverie remembers."
–Gaston Bachelard

do we remember storms or do we imagine them?

if you stand right here   at the top of   Old Hill
you can hear   the wind   un-winding   a myth
it remembers
                blade by blade
                                leaf by leaf
                                    root by root.
then
 the storm   that follows   whirls us together
        in the struggling light.   black feathers
                                                bits of bark

round lyric fruit   gather us   around the fire
of a story.   inside   its hollow bones
the twigs of nests
                        shards of shells and
                                        broken teeth.

(see
the lightning   inside our quivering   blue
souls.   the eyes of children   wide   with
                        what rumbles   in the   blood.

(hear
the thunder   in our starved throats.   borrowed
                words   swirling   in our need.

(listen
how the years of the old ones   open   like flowers
how they turn   into children   let loose
                in fields   of wild weathers.

it is here
        most of us   meet   for the first time.

every day my grandfather walked to his print shop.
sometimes   hand in hand   with my mother.

at five   she knew how to read and write.
to set the letters   neatly
with blackened fingers.   to nest them

            as if   eggs   about to hatch.

                      (I did not know this
                      until I cared.)

at forty
I sent my mother a photo of an old printing press
asked: *was this the type   my grandfather had?*
(the one that made him   the printer of his town.)

the moment I saw it   she said   *I smelled the ink.*

then told me   how
                  this spring
                           she watched
                                        the crows
                              build a nest
            in the linden tree
below our balcony
            as if setting letters
                           for a text
                                    we could learn
                                                to read.

what are these trees?   so gently swaying us
so thin   and delicate like reeds.   humming.

birds   cannot be held within.   such branches
are the scores   of songs
                              that hold us

                                        composed.

                    and the fruit   is   full
of tiny teeth   that get caught between the seeds

like rhymes.

                    crows

                    land   in an uncertainty of twigs.
their nests perched like laughter.   children

swing on vines   back   and forth
high   and low.   without a doubt

in such woods   we grow   we gather
                                        (strong as) weeds.

milk tooth bane bone

I lost my first tooth   at six—
threw it on the roof   for crows
chanting:

here   crow   is my bone tooth!
give me one as strong as iron!

imagined   a crow
lining her nest   with milk teeth.

worried   when   the rains
came down   in torrents:

can a tooth get washed away
before a crow finds it?

but always   a new tooth grew.

*

a child   a crow
and a chant   stretched

  (between them—

a promise one dares
not   to break.

in the little fist— a tooth
in the mouth—   a rhyme:

na ti vrano kosten zoub
dai me ti zhelezen zoub.

a yarn (so fine) around my finger
I wind.   Remember

what holds us   in Time.

*

here   my son sells his tooth to
                              a purple fairy.

                      (a coin

              (a glance

(an innocent exchange in the night.

but I worry
when some haggle   for the price
of this trans-   action.

I gave my teeth   to the crows
and they have not left me   alone.

a book. in its pages   nests   a crow
she feeds her young   on words

so their blue feathers   shine (black).
children hide   the book   in straw

in the (hollow) of a tree   in leaves
under moss.   they know   the words

go missing

                  sometimes   in a blink.

always   fill in   the blanks.

and each time   they   open it
          a crow
                  flies away.

or they keep their stories safe in the Fool's mouth.

his imaginary friends—   deadly beasts
whose bones get picked   so clean

they glisten   with so much   telling.

listen

they eat his babblings   like   hot cakes
take them home   to scare their parents

but the Fool said so   they say.

what makes a man tell a story   over?

the orders crackled through: my great grandfather
was to hold the mountain ridge.
                    buy time   with his *infantry*.

saw   his men die—   one   after
the other.   including his best friend.

he ordered the living   to line up   the dead   just so—
their helmets on   guns pointing   and ready.

every few metres   propped on rocks   trees
—a death chain.

bullets   mortars   shells   begin again.
a few men   flee.   behind them—   fireworks

of flesh   and bone.

at the dinner table   :wide eyed: my dad listens.
the story   always ends:

my best friend   saved   my life.

                              what makes a man

tell a story over   and over?   as if
there is   still   something in it for him
                                        to grasp.

crows in the ruins

the day was not remembered by the sunset—
peach coloured   leaning into night.

on these barren fields   and h*ills*
even vultures would a*void* the carcass of a mind
that has seen too much.

       *

the day was remembered   by what it took away.
always a little sooner   than expected.

around the dinner table—   the silence of mist.

ruins hidden
                    in the eyes of the old ones.

a raucous of crows
                    in the eyes of the young.

       *

we spend most of our days
                    here—
in the middle of

                    (no   time

the clatter   of knives
                    and forks

                    brings us

                    back.

through this door   he said
the cold comes in
slices.   the hunger

in little boxes.   child silhouettes
line up.   hollow   to the world

their hands   wounded crows
their eyes   wild flowers

we do not have to   bury
in our own words   our devices

we do not   have to bury
their eyes   wild flowers

their hands wounded   crows
line up.   hollow   to the world

in little boxes.   child silhouettes
slices.   the hunger

the cold comes in
through this door   he said

the sirens go off.

Grandpa   my father calls. pulls at his sleeves.
we have to get to the shelter.

grandpa will not budge. deaf   he thought
the bombs   were potatoes popping on the stove.

my father runs. climbs down the water meter shaft.
drags the concrete cover   above.
crouches   at the bottom.

when the bombs die down—   pushes   pushes.
but the rubble   piled on top is   too heavy
for seven-year-old shoulders   to lift.

calls.

calls.   till he loses his thin voice.   falls
asleep   straddling the running water below.

they find him   after a day   alive
thanks to a trickle   that brought air into the hole.

months later   he and his friends   play
soldiers   (40some metres from the house)
in the crater where the cigarette factory used to be.

watching out for the snakes   that turned the place home.

a possible expla*nation*

the front part of a crow   comes into
                                        (the picture.
there are no trees   (here.

          among an iteration   of meta pieces
                    the snowflake is   (un-

spoken.
          this place could be   as dry as sawdust   or
as full   as a savannah rain.

who would say

here
          half a woman   will serve you
                    half a bread   on half a scarf.

the other half   (exists in a place
          where blades are   another way

                    of imagining   ourselves
                              bowing in a wind of   steel.

          in the slow fluidity   (of redefining
only numbers are   (whole.

there's no telling
                              how.   to escape
                                        the fire of the half
blade.

          or why when you turn your head
                    after the crow

                    you see it leaving
                                        (with your one eye.

dark clouds   gather   circle
form the eye   of a storm.

so much dust   I cannot tell what
        stands still

        at the centre.

is it words   left out?

black feathers?   bits of bark?   unanswered

questions   claws   or beaks?

what remains after a tree   has bent too far?

the *proof* gone.   what walls are standing
cannot hold   the breath within.

hands turning   black earth. fists
                twisting roots.

on such days   the sun breaks
                  and half of it is the crow

at the top of the willow
            bending the day
                  into the pond's
                              frozen
                                    surface.
this thin
        cracking
              of words.
                    in whose
                          (imagined)
                                depths
                                    we *refine*
darkness.

        out of fear
                swallow
                      its name

when children   hang   in trees   like
pods   waiting to burst
                                   lighter than laughter

the picture is thrown   off balance.

sounds we used to pull   from sure
innocent places   are now   rocks—

each one   with a point   we cling to.

this is why our pictures   hang askew.
we remember   crows   instead of

children.   up there   they hold us
in their eyes.   and when they look away

we fall.

a crow
        lands   on a grey stone:

his afternoon perch   en route to
the other end   of the park.

this stone speaks   of a poet: spent
so much time   in the mountains   that
only a boulder   could do for a grave.

crow knows him well.   visits often.
children here climb   hide   jump   and play.

their laughter   sheds   wild flowers
around the grave.

I have woken up   the crows
their black plumage   fills the air

in an unexpected   narrative
their shadows—   homeless

children   on the playground.
circle   the tree.

they sit   and haggle
fan their tails   bob their heads

hammer out   something
in the back   of their throats.

          (I listen.

in this meadow they stride
          (as if *they*

are the keepers   of the green—
blades   bulbs   even worms

that push up   through such
alluvial   dreams.

in another   wor(l)d the boy will not

give it to the crow   his first tooth.

neither will he lay it under a pillow
in the night.

when it falls out   he will throw it
into the sun.

he smiles at   his crow   on paper.
in his mouth—   a beam of light.

:in the ten *thous*and things:
sm*all* voices

"When the soul lies down in that grass,
the world is too full to talk about.
Ideas, language, even the phrase *each other*
doesn't make any sense."
–Rumi

"I quake to think of you as part of myself
more admissible than grief."
–Alan Davies

the crow hour

last night—   fragments of a dream

wedged themselves   this way   and that

              into some semblance   of

sense.   outside the tent   the wind

forced the lake   against the shore—

              quickened that urgency in dreams.

                          an unrelenting rhythm

bore   through rocks   and pebbles.

              an ungrammatical symphony

of crest and foam   of crash

and roar

              knocking

                    on my existential door.

I step out onto the sand   face this wind

that did not go into a lull   not once.

behind   over my left shoulder—   the crow

watches   me   walking

73

up and down   words   where *I quake.*

so close to what appears   random.

where I *think of you   as part of myself*

            more admissible than   grief.

where I do not want anything   from you

            just everything with you   in it.

this   :all of a sudden: I know.

this   :I am not alone: here.

and poetry?   what can it do

before we awake?

                        but take us   part way

November   (in another year of War

the rains have come   again.
                        boughs
                scold
the wind.

under the skin   in my palms
a quickening—   small red
                birds   taking off.

how the rain   sits
                on crows' wings
                                as they take the place
                        of leaves—

black   in the trees
                        black against   November sky.

these tannin tears   are not
                                what you   (think.

below   the maple leaves
                                claw   the earth—
                        their seven
        little fingers   curling
so unbearably   red

                leaves

on the ground—   thousands
                                        of hearts

                                turning
                        the seasons
                around.

part of my school curriculum included:

how to assemble   a kalashnikov
in less than three minutes

                              then aim.

that was before
we had even learned
to get along   with each other.

                    *

if they asked me now   I would say:

give me words   to assemble.

their triggers   much more sensitive
to where   they fall

what comes after
their small   brilliant explosions.

                              ”It wants a shape inside itself
                         clean enough to lie down with sorrow.”
                                              –Tim Lilburn

between two bridges by the water
I ask the same
question   every day

                         (their faces waiting.
they say it is mist
rolling in from the sea
that turns   this city into

                         (silhouettes and shadows.

the sun   —a moon—   barely
makes an appearance today
even I   can stare at it

                         (with a clear conscience.

the crows on rooftops   grow
impatient
                         (loud

we live beneath   construction
cranes.   suspended in this mist
metaphor   we move words like packages

          packages
                         (like questions.

of the dead
we do not speak   just dream
and hope   we do not see

                         (their faces waiting at the crosswalk.

what holds   (us

I hear the black charred voice of
all the words   from the crowns of trees.

it is here among   *all the silences*
disguised as words   that one raven   speaks

among many   crows.

only the water   *adrift   between us*
reflects.   as we cross   every day

back   and forth
from the city   (its skyline   calligraphy)

to perch   in the stark branches of
                                        memory

and the unsaid.

          where we are
                    blind.

               *

yet
        in between
                    is where   (we hold

        our meaning.

"...even the philosophy of metaphor
is inescapably metaphorical."
–K. Simms

true   or false

in language)   we become   true
or false.   in metaphor   (we encounter

the chaos   (ensuing   from
the flapping of a wing   in the east.

Nietzsche thought   science—
                the cemetery   *of perception.*

Niels Bohr   saw
                the atom   as a drop
of water.

even   *the philosophy*   *of metaphor is*
inescapably   *metaphorical*

to define it   is. to. see   how. close.
we. can.   get. to.   a. bird.

                                        before

                                (it takes off.

words   have   no choice
          in what is sewn   tucked
in their ancestral hems.

                              too burdened
for   the truth

                    full of paper cuts   we flock
under wings   lift off pages

blackened with ink.   curl up
                    in the folds   of cities

the margins of   gutters   and concrete.

and because   I cannot find
the words   to put   :us: in

I must use   the words   that don't

that even the crows   won't   eat.

the crow   by the pond   preens
in the   varied   weathers—

in the rain
            in the sun
                        in the snow.

preens   as if   it thinks   nothing

of the night

            that sleeps on
                        in its feathers.

we weave our destinies   daily
with a scream   and a rattle

a whine and   a coo
a caw   and a cackle.

among the city's neon signs   humming
homing us in.   crooning

from warm beds   from cedar-lined
nests   cradling   speckled eggs.

when we   chopped the trees down
and offered you dumpsters   to dive in

back alleys   to raise your young

what do you choose   to line   your nests with?

I sit under   spring.   under
cherry trees   I know
                        will not bear
                                    fruit.

words tied   in knots.   as if

this is how   we measure thought—
from *not*   to *not*.

every day   here   minding my crows—

determined   velo*cities*   of *sinew*
b*one*   fe*at*her   *claw*.

a take off re*gist*ers in the aperture of a puddle
our g*lances* d*art* through crisp air.

                              exchange gifts.

something simmers   in the eye
        boils over
                the copper edge
                    of the horizon.

lifts.

they appear like they have a mind of their own
these conversations—   wild birds

we read.   an exchange across generations.
lured   for a while   we share word trays.

peck   side   by side.
never having met.

                              it is late where you are
and I have a whole day   ahead of me.

who will enter?   there is no telling.
          what comes next?

no logic.   surely   no waste either.

you say   to us it makes no sense   but
who are we?   what is   our
                                        sense?

these days
I a*void*   writing the trains of

logic.   winter fields
                  reasoning

between frames.
            we are axioms of sky.

lymph   in sorrow.   mourning

our damp doubt.   permeable
        membranes of   word.clouds

consonants   as if.
            caught missing

in the hands of gravity   turning snow.

look   how we bind   Now
how it falls   against
          the mind's blade

dissecting
      atoms   flakes   flesh   bone.
               so little

        can
        :blind us:

we change our minds as to how we feel about you.
we call   you

                              pest   or *helper*

survivor   or *predator*

lofty messenger   or *noisy trash bird*

enigma

                    shape-shifter

                                        problem solver.

scavenger   or *creator of the world.*

you hop out of the field   into the fable
and back.

                              you permeate our stories
not because   we have   you figured out

but because   we haven't.

on the porch of   the moment
we *swing*   back   and forth

stitching a hem   through time

christmas tree tinsel   kite strings
dental floss   newspapers   yarn

building nests
                tucking in   stories.

"For a dreamer, a dreamer of words, they
are all swollen with insanities."
–Gaston Bachelard

again   here come the crows

                    (my poem

(my experiment

                  in freedom.

suspicious of words   I shift
     within.   their premises   I walk.

as the age turns on its contra-

                  dictions.

bent   on gathering intelligence.
calculating   *collateral* damage.

here come the crows   to peck my flesh.

I couldn't be?

        could I   possibly?

        would I know

    if I was

dead?

*

or sleeping
            inside   the shiny mussel eye

        within the poem
                (its contra-   dictions.

the age grinds back   on its experiment
spreads   its pitch tar   wings

its far reaching   spiritual blackout

inside my premises.   I walk
shift   swarms of
                suspicious

        words

that only for an instant   line up
        in the tangle   of my senses

                my intuition.

and here lies the skeleton   of the poem
what is left
                              is

                                        what is wanted

bones   picked   *clean*
bleached   against   river rocks.

each vertebrae—   an instant   that can
stick   in the throat   of thought.

another flies   through—   a moment
I had   forgotten.   the *swish* of

its wings—   the sound of   my hand
                     (two st/r\okes   on paper.

crow   clouds   gather
grow   in winter   light

down by the great chestnut
creaking   with senseless wind

you   and I
eating   first   snow

after so many mea*sure*d words   he said:

walk
          with your bare feet
                         on the earth.

by the edge of the water she said:

o*pen* each word
                as if it is
                              a hand-

kerchief   wrapped   around bread.

                   and you are hungry.

at the dinner table—   bowls of piping soup.
a letter for a beak.   a seed   for an eye.

watches.   blue breath quivers   in black
feathers.   we *share* myths   with half-

imagined birds. recount cups of losses
tablespoons of pain.   knead tales with

flour.   break bread with each other.

break the surface

                              of the everyday

                  for what   *drifts*

            dreams

under.

there are no recipes   for getting to
                                 know you.

fascination aside:
                        today   every sound
that comes out of you

                        grates   on my ear.

I try to ignore you   better.

                   unwilling to listen
                                 I do.

I want to be
               composed
                   as you
                          in the rain.

comfortable
              as you
                       in the city.

inscribed
              as you
                   in the landscape.

the light in your eyes
              has taken *years*
                     to reach me

it is not like we have ever been able to talk.
still   here   eye to eye   we exist

in this—   our crowsmos.

where   we turn our heads
after each other   at tension

and cannot say   why.

where   we hold   each other   in the eye
as if we are   lovers.

            have something to give.

each look

            drops

                a star

                    in my lap.

the clouds this morning for the first time in days
parted
         let the sun through

broke the sky into   rags   of blue.
clouds caught   in winter boughs.

the crow preens feather   after feather
takes its time   as the vast firmament slips through

these branching syllables.   our hands too
reaching up   grasping   at world

morphologies.   these trees   we analyse
upside down.

      the scarf around your neck
          bluer than blue.

and if you lie   here
in the *shallows*   of summer

so still   the *years* grow
as sharp   as grass.

r e m e m b   e   r   i   n   g
through your   startled limbs.

you think   it's wind.   but
what holds us   here   pinned

by shooting August stars

                  are echoes

                        calling us

                              by name.

:post*script*:

"How can anyone say what happens, even if each of us
dips a pen a hundred million times into ink?"
–Rumi

> "So what if the gods of these poems no longer come to visit me?/
> This book is where they make their home,/flying to and fro in its pages/
> depending on whose eyes are near."
> –Pain Not Bread

So what if   the [crows]   *of these poems*
no longer come   to visit me?

words are   lumps   of coal
come   alive.   they spread their wings
and fly off   into the night

leaving

        something small   and shiny
in the mind.

                          for now

this book is where they make   *their home*
flying to   and fro

in its pages.   celestial shivers
where   the maple leaves   become hands
the stone—   living   breathing tissue.

        *

in these pages   we exist
because   we strongly believe   we can

                *

even though   we no longer   remember

        how

                    *

                to go home.

<h1 style="text-align:center">:acknowledgements:</h1>

The seeds were planted more than a decade ago. Three people accompanied me on this journey at different times of the incubation and writing. My gratitude goes to:

Harold Rhenisch for helping with the initial edits as poems were coming into being. (The title of the poem "milk tooth bane bone" emerged at that time and later became the title of the book.) Aislinn Hunter for taking me with grace and tight reins through the final versions/edits of the manuscript. Also for the welcoming hand of an introduction she wrote to the book.

Ursula Vaira for spending time with my crows, for recognizing them, for giving them a home here. I thrive on your encouragement, trust and support.

I am grateful for the support of the BC Arts Council during the writing of the book.

The book would not be what it is if it were not for the Vancouver crows, for their relentless call and daily reminders to attend to them, no matter what the season. You have been a most dedicated muse.

The poem on page 68 refers to a real boulder which was brought down from Vitosha Mountain to mark the grave of Bulgarian poet, novelist and playwright, Ivan Vazov (1850–1921). It is located in a small city park in the centre of Sofia near the church St. Sophia. I would like to acknowledge my indebtedness to the Bulgarian poets/writers, who were also revolutionaries, who dedicated their genius and their lives in the fight for freedom. Through their words, through my skin.

The title "the crow hour" came from a conversation with Wayde Compton. He and his daughter, Senna, stumbled on great numbers of crows at the Strathcona Community Garden on an early summer evening. The crow hour was the name they gave for that time when the crows would congregate and Senna would see them again. I dedicate this poem to her.

Thank you to the editors of the following journals/magazines/ anthologies where earlier versions of some of the poems here originally appeared:

In print: *Vallum, Environmental Philosophy Journal, Arabesque Review, filling Station, Poiesis, The Pinnacle* and *Rocksalt: an Anthology of Contemporary BC Poetry* (Mother Tongue Publishing, 2008).

Online: *Paideusis, Contemporary Verse 2, Arabesque Review, ditch, Blue Print Review, educational insights, qarrtsiluni, The Incongruous Quarterly* and *filling Station.*

The poem that begins "between two bridges by the water" appeared under the title "dying for answers" in my previous poetry collection, *the weight of dew* (Mother Tongue Publishing, 2012).

Thank you Frank Lee for taking my photo. Sending my photos out is a lot less anxious of an experience now.

I extend my gratitude further to the people in my poetry/ writing community who have published my work, have nurtured it, who have shared kind words, believe in what I do and have not hesitated to let me know. They may not have had direct connection to this book, but I also believe things are more connected than we let them be. In no specific order, thank you to Mona Fertig, Arlene Ang, Kate Braid, Lorri Neilsen Glenn, George McWhirter, Valerie Fox, Renée Saklikar, Alan Twigg, Zsuzsi Gartner, Dave Bonta, Betsy Warland, Rob Taylor, Evelyn Lau, Christina Shah, Dr. James Hatley, Trevor Carolan, William Welton, Dr. Heesoon Bai, Elee Kraljii Gardiner, Dr. Celeste Snowber, Kim Clark, Dr. Carl Leggo, Bonnie Nish, Christi Kramer, Dr. Lynn Fels, Heidi Greco, Catherine Owen, Melinda Cochrane, Al Rempel, Jude Neale, Robin Susanto, Dana Guthrie Martin, just to mention a few.

To musicians Clyde Reed and Jared Burrows for lending their music to my words, thank you. To the two people who gave

me a standing ovation at my reading last year at the
Summer Dream Literary Arts Festival, thank you.

As always, I am grateful for the strength that comes
from friends and family, from my parents, my aunt,
the inspiration that comes from my children and my
husband, Dethe—your support is an everyday blessing.

The book cover comes from a canvas my son painted. It
is no secret I am a fan of art created by young people.

Last but not least, to you the reader, thank you.

:notes:

The quotes in the introduction by Aislinn Hunter come
from the following two texts: *A Short History of Myth*,
by Karen Armstrong, Alfred A. Knopf, Toronto, 2005;
and *Nine Gates: Entering the Mind of Poetry by* Jane
Hirshfield, Harper Perennial, New York, 1998.

Epigraphs in order of appearance (with thanks):

The epigraph by Rainer Maria Rilke comes from his
"First Duino Elegy" in *The Selected Poetry of Rainer
Maria Rilke* (Stephen Mitchell, Trans.), Vintage Books,
1989.

13 The epigraph by Lyubomir Levchev comes from his
poem "Semantic Seeds" in *Ashes of Light,* Curbstone
Press, 2006.

17 The epigraph "Language is what something becomes
when you think in it" comes from Robert Bringhurst's
essay "Poetry and Thinking" in *Thinking and Singing:
Poetry and the Practice of Philosophy* (Tim Lilburn, Ed.),
Cormorant Books, 2002.

25 The epigraph "As the eye cannot see itself directly/But
only in reflection/So also does consciousness appear/

Mirrored in the ten thousand things" I believe comes from Lao Tzu, but have not been able to track it down. Oh, the imperfection of memory.

28 The epigraph by Ross Leckie comes from the poem "The Critique of Pure Reason" published in *The Malahat Review*, Fall 2009, No. 168.

51 The epigraph by Aislinn Hunter comes from her poem "A Last Letter from Your Most Affectionate, Anon" in *The Possible Past*, Polestar and Raincoast Books, 2004.

52 The phrase "the memory dreams, and reverie remembers" comes from Gaston Bachelard's *The Poetics of Reverie: Childhood, Language and the Cosmos* (M. Jolas, Trans.), Beacon Press, 1969.

69 Goethe's "One must ask children and birds how cherries and strawberries taste" comes from "Bias Is the Nose of the Story" by Gerald Smallberg in *This Will Make You Smarter* (John Brockman, Ed.), HarperCollins Publishers, 2012.

71 The epigraph by Rumi comes from *The Essential Rumi* (Coleman Barks, Trans.), HarperCollins, 2010.

73 The epigraph by Alan Davies comes from *Active 24 Hours*, The Segue Foundation, 1982.

77 The epigraph by Tim Lilburn comes from *To the River*, McClelland & Stewart, 1999.

78 The epigraph "All the words, all the silences disguised/ as words, adrift between us and the unsaid" comes from Robert Bringhurst's poem "Absence of the Heart" in *Selected Poems*, Gaspereau Press, 2009.

79 The phrase "even the philosophy of metaphor is inescapably metaphorical" comes from K. Simms in *Paul Ricoeur*, Routledge, 2003.

88　The epigraph "For a dreamer, a dreamer of words, they are all swollen with insanities" comes from Gaston Bachelard's *The Poetics of Reverie: Childhood, Language and the Cosmos* (M. Jolas, Trans.), Beacon Press, 1969.

96　The epigraph by Martin Heidegger comes from "The Thinker as Poet" in *Poetry, Language, Thought* (Albert Hofstadter, trans.), HarperCollins Publishers, 1971.

99　The epigraph by Rumi is from *The Essential Rumi* (Coleman Barks, Trans.), HarperCollins, 2010.

101　The epigraph by Pain Not Bread comes from the poem "Scraps of Paper (From the Late Tang)" in *Introduction to the Introduction to Wang Wei*, Brick Books, 2000.

Daniela Elza has lived on three continents and crossed numerous geographic, cultural and semantic borders. Her work has appeared in over sixty publications both at home and internationally. In 2011 Daniela received her doctorate in Philosophy of Education from Simon Fraser University and launched her first e-Book, *The Book of It.* Daniela's thesis, toward a *Pedagogy of the Imagination,* was nominated for a 2011 distinguished dissertation award from the Canadian Association for Graduate Studies and in 2012 was awarded the Dean of Graduate Studies Convocation Medal. Daniela's debut poetry collection, *the weight of dew,* was published in 2012 by Mother Tongue Publishing. Daniela lives with her family in Vancouver, BC.